MAGIC TREE HOUSE®

incredible fact book

What in the world is a dementor wasp?

Turn to page 20 to find out!

MAGIC TREE HOUSE® BOOKS

#1: DINOSAURS BEFORE DARK
#2: THE KNIGHT AT DAWN
#3: MUMMIES IN THE MORNING
#4: PIRATES PAST NOON
#5: NIGHT OF THE NINJAS
#6: AFTERNOON ON THE AMAZON
#7: SUNSET OF THE SABERTOOTH
#8: MIDNIGHT ON THE MOON
#9: DOLPHINS AT DAYBREAK
#10: GHOST TOWN AT SUNDOWN
#11: LIONS AT LUNCHTIME
#12: POLAR BEARS PAST BEDTIME
#13: VACATION UNDER THE VOLCANO
#14: DAY OF THE DRAGON KING
#15: VIKING SHIPS AT SUNRISE
#16: HOUR OF THE OLYMPICS
#17: TONIGHT ON THE *TITANIC*
#18: BUFFALO BEFORE BREAKFAST
#19: TIGERS AT TWILIGHT
#20: DINGOES AT DINNERTIME
#21: CIVIL WAR ON SUNDAY
#22: REVOLUTIONARY WAR ON WEDNESDAY
#23: TWISTER ON TUESDAY
#24: EARTHQUAKE IN THE EARLY MORNING
#25: STAGE FRIGHT ON A SUMMER NIGHT
#26: GOOD MORNING, GORILLAS
#27: THANKSGIVING ON THURSDAY
#28: HIGH TIDE IN HAWAII

MERLIN MISSIONS

#29: CHRISTMAS IN CAMELOT
#30: HAUNTED CASTLE ON HALLOWS EVE
#31: SUMMER OF THE SEA SERPENT
#32: WINTER OF THE ICE WIZARD
#33: CARNIVAL AT CANDLELIGHT
#34: SEASON OF THE SANDSTORMS
#35: NIGHT OF THE NEW MAGICIANS
#36: BLIZZARD OF THE BLUE MOON
#37: DRAGON OF THE RED DAWN
#38: MONDAY WITH A MAD GENIUS
#39: DARK DAY IN THE DEEP SEA
#40: EVE OF THE EMPEROR PENGUIN
#41: MOONLIGHT ON THE MAGIC FLUTE
#42: A GOOD NIGHT FOR GHOSTS
#43: LEPRECHAUN IN LATE WINTER
#44: A GHOST TALE FOR CHRISTMAS TIME
#45: A CRAZY DAY WITH COBRAS
#46: DOGS IN THE DEAD OF NIGHT
#47: ABE LINCOLN AT LAST!
#48: A PERFECT TIME FOR PANDAS
#49: STALLION BY STARLIGHT
#50: HURRY UP, HOUDINI!
#51: HIGH TIME FOR HEROES
#52: SOCCER ON SUNDAY

#53: SHADOW OF THE SHARK
#54: BALTO OF THE BLUE DAWN
#55: NIGHT OF THE NINTH DRAGON

SUPER EDITIONS

DANGER IN THE DARKEST HOUR

MAGIC TREE HOUSE® FACT TRACKERS

DINOSAURS
KNIGHTS AND CASTLES
MUMMIES AND PYRAMIDS
PIRATES
RAIN FORESTS
SPACE
TITANIC
TWISTERS AND OTHER TERRIBLE STORMS
DOLPHINS AND SHARKS
ANCIENT GREECE AND THE OLYMPICS
AMERICAN REVOLUTION
SABERTOOTHS AND THE ICE AGE
PILGRIMS
ANCIENT ROME AND POMPEII
TSUNAMIS AND OTHER NATURAL DISASTERS
POLAR BEARS AND THE ARCTIC
SEA MONSTERS
PENGUINS AND ANTARCTICA
LEONARDO DA VINCI
GHOSTS
LEPRECHAUNS AND IRISH FOLKLORE
RAGS AND RICHES: KIDS IN THE TIME OF CHARLES DICKENS
SNAKES AND OTHER REPTILES
DOG HEROES
ABRAHAM LINCOLN
PANDAS AND OTHER ENDANGERED SPECIES
HORSE HEROES
HEROES FOR ALL TIMES
SOCCER
NINJAS AND SAMURAI
CHINA: LAND OF THE EMPEROR'S GREAT WALL
SHARKS AND OTHER PREDATORS
VIKINGS
DOGSLEDDING AND EXTREME SPORTS
DRAGONS AND MYTHICAL CREATURES

MORE MAGIC TREE HOUSE®

GAMES AND PUZZLES FROM THE TREE HOUSE
MAGIC TRICKS FROM THE TREE HOUSE
MY MAGIC TREE HOUSE JOURNAL
MAGIC TREE HOUSE SURVIVAL GUIDE
ANIMAL GAMES AND PUZZLES
MAGIC TREE HOUSE INCREDIBLE FACT BOOK

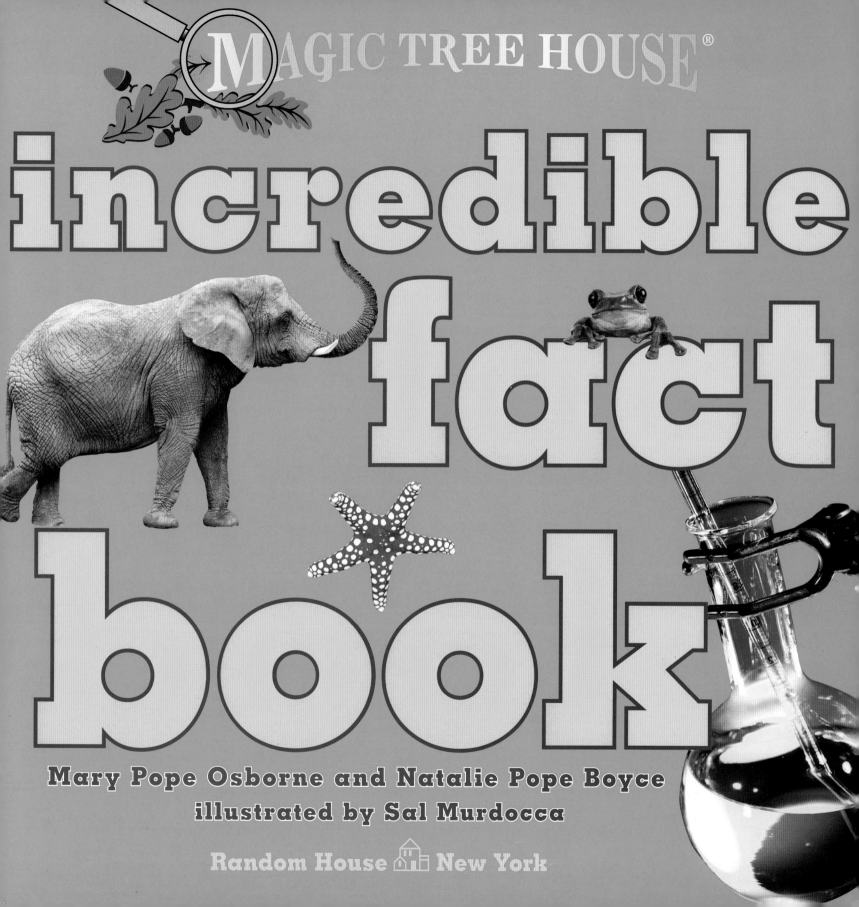

MAGIC TREE HOUSE®

incredible fact book

Mary Pope Osborne and Natalie Pope Boyce

illustrated by Sal Murdocca

Random House 🏠 New York

Text copyright © 2016 by Mary Pope Osborne and Natalie Pope Boyce

Cover art and new colorized illustrations copyright © 2016 by Sal Murdocca

Cover photograph credits: © Potapov Alexander/Shutterstock (skeleton); © blickwinkel/Alamy Stock Photo (frog); © MarcelClemens/Shutterstock (Jupiter); © Reinhard Dirscherl/Alamy Stock Photo (squid); © Cathy Keifer/Shutterstock (sundew with fly); © Levent Konuk/Shutterstock (soccer ball); © Masyanya/Shutterstock (Leaning Tower of Pisa); © PRILL/Shutterstock (rocket); © Somchai Som/Shutterstock (Earth); © Kuttelvaserova Stuchelova/Shutterstock (chameleon)

Random House and the colophon are registered trademarks of Penguin Random House LLC.

Magic Tree House is a registered trademark of Mary Pope Osborne; used under license.

Visit us on the Web!

randomhousekids.com

MagicTreeHouse.com

Educators and librarians, for a variety of teaching tools, visit us at RHTeachersLibrarians.com

Library of Congress Cataloging-in-Publication Data is available upon request.

ISBN 978-0-399-55117-8 (trade) — ISBN 978-0-399-55118-5 (lib. bdg.) —
ISBN 978-0-399-55134-5 (ebook)

MANUFACTURED IN CHINA

10 9 8 7 6 5 4 3 2

First Edition

CONTENTS

Dear Readers,

The magic tree house has taken us all over the world! We've gone back in time to see the dinosaurs. We've met Abraham Lincoln and sailed on the <u>Titanic</u>. We've been to ancient Egypt and Greece and China and Japan.

When we come back from an adventure, we like to track the facts about the times and places we've visited. We go to the library and check out books. We search on the Internet. And of course, we always write down cool, interesting facts in our notebook. As you can imagine, we've collected a <u>lot</u> of facts—and we can't wait to share the best ones with you!

This book is full of our very favorite facts about all kinds of stuff. Some of them are really gross. Many of them surprise and impress us. All of them remind us of what a strange and fascinating world we live in.

Prepare to be amazed!

Jack Annie

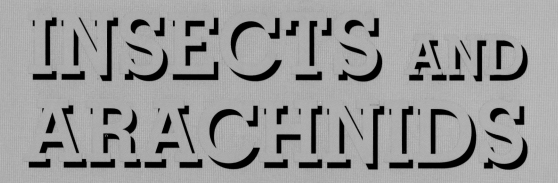

INSECTS AND ARACHNIDS

Bees, butterflies, and houseflies are just a few of the million different kinds of insects.

All insects have **SIX** legs. Most go through four stages of life—egg, larva, pupa, and adult.

Did you know that insects are animals?

Spiders aren't insects. They are animals called *arachnids* (uh-RAK-nids). **ARACHNID** is a Greek word for *spider*.

Arachnids have eight legs. **TICKS,** mites, scorpions, and spiders are arachnids.

The **MOST DANGEROUS ANIMAL** in the world is the mosquito. Mosquitoes can carry deadly diseases like malaria and yellow fever. Malaria alone kills over 600,000 people a year. (Sharks kill an average of ten.)

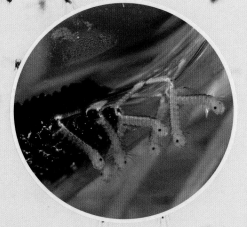

MOSQUITOES lay their eggs in water. Even a little puddle will do. If you want to cut down on the number of mosquitoes in your yard, try to get rid of standing water. Empty your birdbaths, flowerpots, or anything else that can collect rainwater.

There are three ways mosquitoes find people or animals. They can see motion. They can detect infrared radiation, which all warm-blooded animals give off. They are attracted to the carbon dioxide we exhale and other chemicals in our bodies. Some species of mosquitoes are even attracted to **STINKY FEET!**

Mosquitoes don't sting. They don't really bite, either. They don't even have teeth! They stab you with their needle-like snouts and then drink your **BLOOD.** They can hold up to three times their body weight in blood.

MALE mosquitoes don't drink blood. They live on plant nectar. But watch out for those females!

A male mosquito's wings beat **550 TO 650 TIMES** every second. Females' wings beat 350 to 450 times. It's the mosquito's beating wings that make that buzzing sound.

It drives me crazy, especially when I'm trying to sleep!

A beehive might have as many as 65,000 bees in it.

Bees are the only insects that create food that humans can eat—honey. First, worker bees suck up nectar from flowers and store it in a special stomach called the honey stomach. Then they throw up the nectar and give it to other bees in the hive. Those bees chew it and throw it up a few more times before they deposit it in the hive. Then it's **HONEY!**

Bees fly about **SIXTY MILES** a day. They must gather nectar from over 400 flowers to make just one tablespoon of honey. But they have to work together. Most bees make only one-twelfth of a teaspoon of honey in their life. While bees gather nectar, pollen attaches to their legs. Insects pollinate 80 percent of all crops.

The sweat bee of America is one of the few bees that can **FLY IN THE DARK.** It finds its way by memorizing landmarks near the hive.

Bees fly faster when they go with the wind rather than against it. ● Honeybees have very fine hairs on their eyes that tell them which direction the wind is blowing. ● Bees sting more often on windy days.

The **DEAD LEAF MANTIS** of Malaysia is almost impossible to see. It is the exact color of a dried-out brown leaf.

A fly's eyes, brain, and muscles are so closely connected that it can sense **DANGER** almost immediately. That's why it's so hard to swat a pesky fly! Houseflies can walk upside down on a ceiling because their feet are sticky.

Some insects and earthworms have **GREEN BLOOD.** This is because of the color of the plants they eat.

A flea can jump **50 TO 100 TIMES** higher than the length of its body. An average eight-year-old girl is about four feet tall. If she could jump like a flea, she would go over 400 feet in one leap.

That's longer than a football field!

There are over 10,000 different kinds of ants around the world.

● Ants can live underwater for two days. ● Ants communicate by sending out special chemical smells to let other ants know where to find food, where to build new nests, and when there is danger. ● Ants have antennae on their heads to gather information about smells, temperature, and sounds. ● Fire ants have ten to twenty different smell signals.

In case of flood, fire ants quickly pile on top of each other to make floating rafts with their bodies. They can **SURVIVE** like this for several days.

The goliath bird-eating tarantula of South America is the **BIGGEST** spider of all. Its legs and body measure almost a foot, and it can weigh up to half a pound. The goliath rarely eats birds. It mostly eats earthworms and toads.

Spiders inject venom into their victims with their two front fangs.

Mexican fishing spiders attach themselves to leaves and float over the water, **PREYING** on small fish and tadpoles. When they feel the vibration of a small fish or tadpole, they race across the surface of the water and grab it.

The Brazilian wandering spider has the **DEADLIEST** venom of all spiders.

Female black widow spiders are **VENOMOUS.** Males are not.

Beetles have been on Earth about 700,000 years.

The Hercules beetle can lift **EIGHTY TIMES** its body weight.

Some beetles, like fireflies, are bioluminescent. This means that their bodies **LIGHT UP** in the dark. A firefly's flashing lights tell other fireflies that it is looking for a mate.

Dung beetles spend their days rolling balls of **MANURE** to their burrows to feed their young.

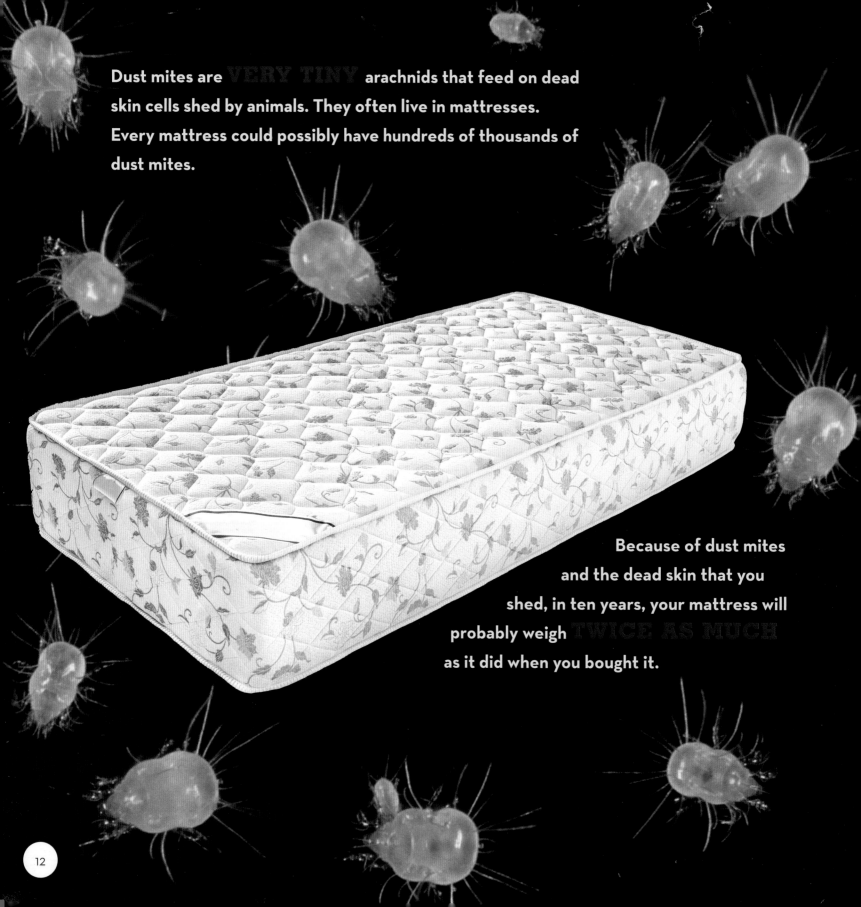

Dust mites are VERY TINY arachnids that feed on dead skin cells shed by animals. They often live in mattresses. Every mattress could possibly have hundreds of thousands of dust mites.

Because of dust mites and the dead skin that you shed, in ten years, your mattress will probably weigh TWICE AS MUCH as it did when you bought it.

Cockroaches have been around for millions of years.

It's difficult to poison a cockroach. It can **TASTE** something without eating it. Cockroaches use hairs on their legs to taste.

The **FOSSIL** of a very large cockroach that lived 300 million years ago was found in a coal mine in Ohio.

Butterflies live on every continent except Antarctica.

Sometimes the bright colors of a butterfly seem to change as it flutters its wings. This **IRIDESCENT** color comes from the scales on its wings.

The Queen Alexandra's birdwing butterfly of New Guinea is the **LARGEST** butterfly. Its wings are over ten and a half inches wide.

● There are about 165,000 different kinds of butterflies. Some live as long as eleven months, while others die after only two weeks. ● Monarch butterflies fly south for the winter. Some travel 265 miles a day and can cover a total of 3,000 miles. No one is exactly sure how monarchs find their way from the United States down to the jungles of Mexico. ● Butterflies taste with their feet. They breathe through openings in their abdomens.

POISON AND VENOM

There are many poisonous and venomous animals in addition to spiders. Both venom and poison are harmful chemicals that can kill people and other animals. Poison enters the body through the skin and mouth. Venom enters the body through bites, stabs, or stings.

The golden dart frog of South America is one of the most **POISONOUS** creatures on Earth. But if you take a golden dart frog out of its habitat, it becomes harmless. The poison comes from the insects it eats in the wild.

The male platypus has venom in his feet. He stings other males during mating season.

● Pitohui birds of New Guinea have a poison much like dart frog's.
If you take away the beetles they eat, they're no longer poisonous.
● There's a venomous frog in Brazil that butts victims with its head.
Tiny spikes on its forehead deliver the venom.

A ribbon worm sticks out its feeding tube to cover its prey in a slimy, smelly, toxic mucus. Yuck!

Stonefish live around coral reefs in the Pacific. They look like stones or a piece of the reef. But watch out! These deadly creatures have sharp spines on their backs loaded with **TOXINS** that can kill a human in two hours.

Some sea snakes have venom more **DEADLY** than a cobra's. Three drops are enough to kill eight people.

Spitting cobras have great aim. They shoot venom from their fangs right into the eyes of their victims, blinding them.

The longest of all venomous snakes is the **KING COBRA.** It can be over eighteen feet. Without treatment, humans will stop breathing thirty minutes after being bitten by a king cobra.

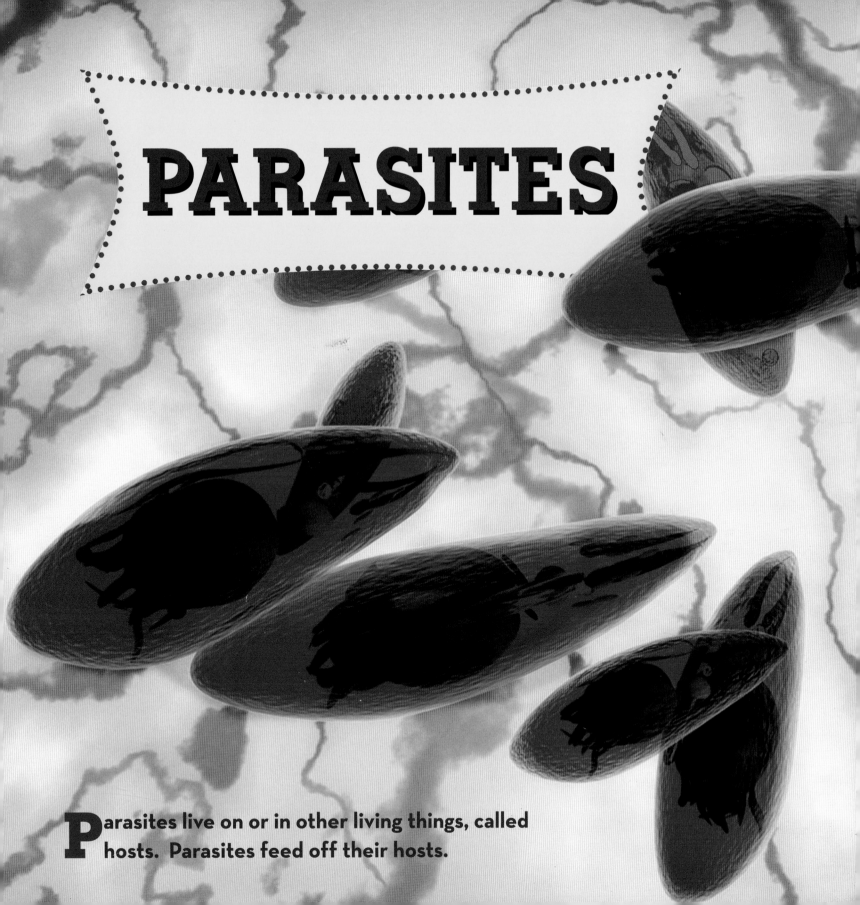

PARASITES

Parasites live on or in other living things, called
hosts. Parasites feed off their hosts.

The horsehair worm lives in water. When a cricket or grasshopper drinks water where the worm lives, it ingests its larva. The larva grows into a worm **FOUR TIMES LONGER** than the insect. The worm controls the insect's brain, and it jumps into water and drowns. Now the worm can live out its adult life in the water.

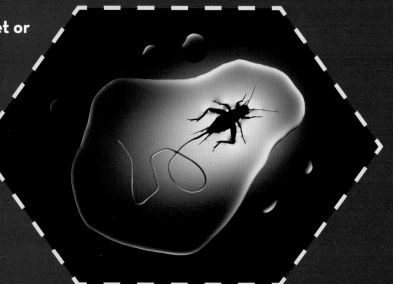

● Rats and mice sometimes get a parasite that causes them to be attracted to cats. And that makes the cats very happy. ● There's a little fly that deposits its eggs in a bee's abdomen and makes the bee act like a zombie. It'll stagger around, try to fly at night, and hang out under streetlights. ● There is a parasite that causes ants to climb to the top of plants at night. This is something they wouldn't normally do. If a cow comes along and eats the plant, the parasite travels to the cow's stomach and lives out the rest of its life there.

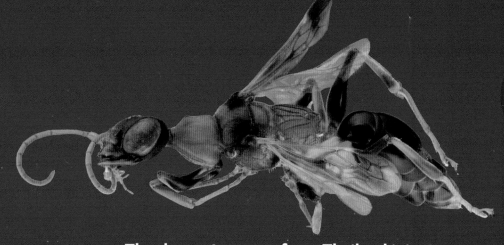

This gives the wasp a chance to drag the cockroach away and eat it in safety.

The dementor wasp from Thailand injects cockroaches with **VENOM** that affects their brains and makes them unable to control their movements.

The **TONGUE-EATING LOUSE** crawls inside a fish through its gills. It cuts off the blood flow to the fish's tongue, and the tongue falls off. Then it grabs on to the stub and acts like a new tongue!

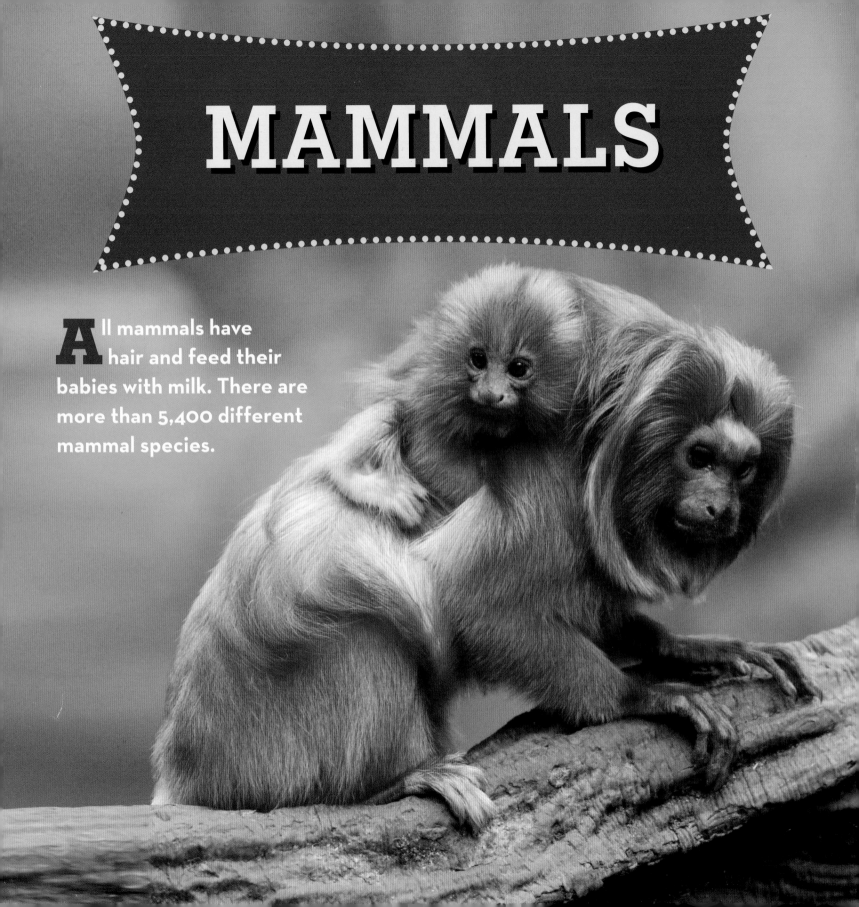

MAMMALS

All mammals have hair and feed their babies with milk. There are more than 5,400 different mammal species.

When snub-nose monkeys in the eastern Himalayan Mountains look up at the rain, water gets in their noses and makes them **SNEEZE.** So when it begins to pour, the monkeys sit quietly with their heads between their legs.

These are Yunnan snub-nosed monkeys, which are closely related to the rare sneezy species.

Chimpanzees use **TOOLS.** They catch termites with sticks and smash nuts with rocks.

Elephants can smell water from three miles away.

Elephants blow dust and mud on their bodies to **PROTECT** themselves from the sun.

● Adult elephants eat up to 400 pounds of food each day. ● Adult male elephants live alone. Female elephants live in groups. The oldest female is the boss. The females in the group babysit and protect each other's babies. ● Elephants are scared of bees. ● When an elephant gets sick, the other elephants bring it food and help it stand up. ● Elephants are very good swimmers. They use their trunks like snorkels to breathe underwater.

Elephants say **HELLO** by wrapping their trunks around each other.

• Lions, tigers, cheetahs, and pet cats belong to the cat family. • There are forty-one different species of cats. • Cats' back paws step almost exactly where their front paws have stepped. This helps them walk so quietly that they can sneak up on their prey. • Evidence shows that people started training cats as pets 12,000 years ago. • Cheetahs don't growl; they bark and make other noises. • Tigers usually hunt at night. • No two tigers have exactly the same stripes. • You can hear a tiger roaring from two miles away. • Bengal tigers of India are great swimmers. They sneak up behind fishermen and snatch them right off their boats. • Female lions do most of the hunting. Males guard their territory and sleep. • Only male lions have manes. But male lions in Tsavo National Park in Kenya and Senegalese lions don't have manes at all. • In ancient Egypt, cats were thought to bring luck. Anyone who killed one could be put to death. • Cheetahs can run at speeds of sixty to seventy miles per hour. That makes them the fastest land animal. • Lions sleep between sixteen and twenty hours a day.

Tigers often lick themselves and their fellow tigers. Their saliva is antiseptic and helps **HEAL** scratches and cuts.

There are more **PET CATS** in the United States than dogs.

Pure white blue-eyed cats are usually **DEAF.**

Polar bears are the largest bears.

● Males can weigh over 1,500 pounds and be over ten feet tall when standing. ● Polar bears can smell a seal that is twenty miles away. ● Polar bears have huge paws—up to a foot across! This helps distribute their weight when they cross thin ice.

Polar bears don't have white hair. Their hair is transparent, or clear. Hollow tubes in each hair reflect the light, making the hair appear to be white.

Gorillas are **PEACEFUL,** shy animals. They are apes, not monkeys. Apes do not have tails. They are larger than most monkeys.

A male gorilla is usually over five feet tall and weighs 400 pounds.

Gorillas **SCARE AWAY** their enemies by standing upright, screaming, roaring, and slapping or pounding their chests.

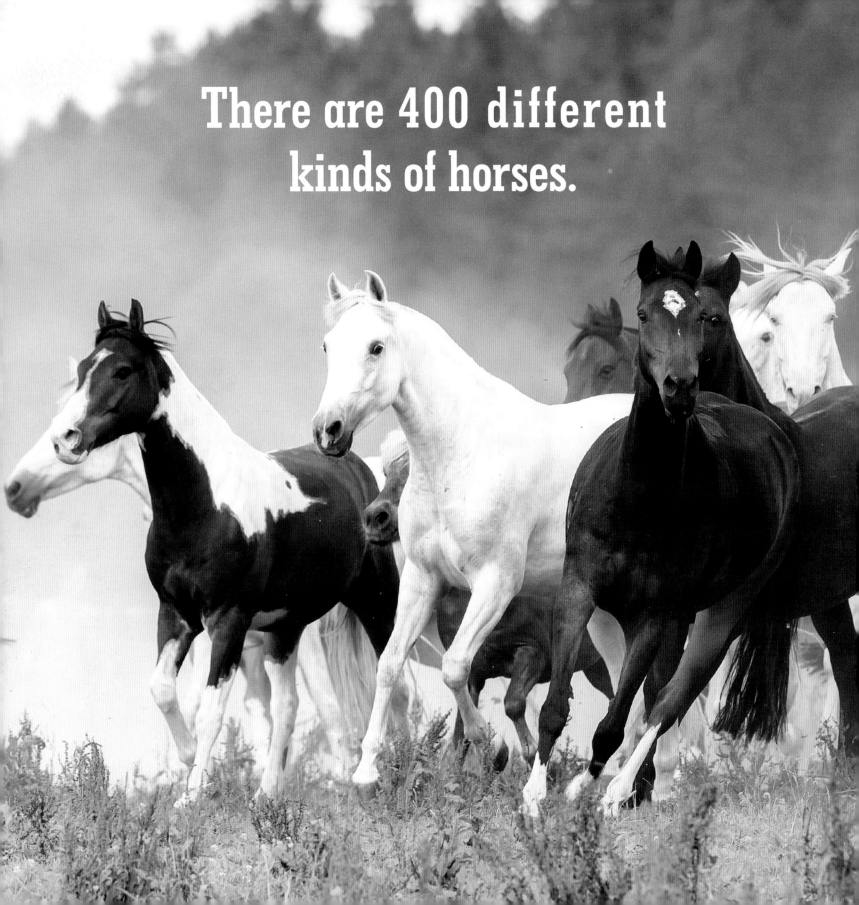

There are 400 different kinds of horses.

Horses walk on their **TIPTOES.**
They don't have muscles below their knees.

- Horses sleep both standing up and lying down.
- A horse has such a small stomach that it has to eat most of the day. ● When a horse is running fast, it breathes in over 264 gallons of air each minute.
- Horses can't breathe through their mouths like we do. They breathe only through their noses.

Some horses can run thirty miles per hour for short periods of time.

Giraffes are the tallest animals on the planet.

Believe it or not, giraffes have the same number of bones in their necks as humans do. Like all mammals, they have seven. In giraffes, each neck bone is about **TEN INCHES LONG.**

Males can be eighteen feet tall.

Giraffes sleep as little as twenty minutes a day.

Giraffes are so tall that it's hard for them to bend down and drink water. Luckily for them, giraffes can go without water for two weeks. That's longer than a camel! Then they will drink about **TWELVE GALLONS** at one time. A giraffe also gets some of its water from the plants it eats.

When it comes to not drinking water, kangaroo rats are the champions. They live years without it.

All dogs are descended from gray wolves.

Dogs can understand up to 200 words. Their noses are **100,000 TIMES** more powerful than humans'. Some dogs have learned to sniff out certain kinds of cancer. Others can alert someone who is about to have an epileptic seizure.

Humans and dogs have lived together for over **12,000 YEARS.**

BIRDS

Most birds' bones are light and hollow. That's one reason they can fly.

Peregrine falcons are the fastest animals on the planet. They can fly 240 miles per hour.

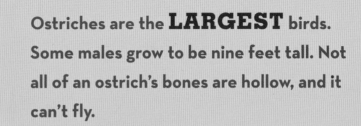

Ostriches are the **LARGEST** birds. Some males grow to be nine feet tall. Not all of an ostrich's bones are hollow, and it can't fly.

Hummingbirds fly over fifteen miles per hour. They are the only birds that can fly backward.

The **SMALLEST** bird is the bee hummingbird. It measures just a little over two inches long. A hummingbird breathes more than 250 times a minute.

Owls **CAN'T MOVE** their eyes. They have to turn their heads to see right and left.

There are around **200 DIFFERENT** owl species.

Owls eat small animals. They digest the meat and spit up the hair and bones. The remains are called an **OWL PELLET.**

Oh, man! I can see the bones!

Because they eat pink krill, Adélie penguins produce **PINK POOP.** They track it all over the ice, and the ice turns pink as well. It can even be seen from space.

The Emperor penguin is the tallest of all penguin species, reaching as much as **FORTY-SEVEN** inches tall.

Like all penguins, Adélies are built for **SWIMMING,** not flying.

Little blue penguins are the **SMALLEST** penguins. They are about thirteen inches tall.

SEA CREATURES

There are more than 200,000 animal species in the oceans of the world. Scientists think there could be up to a million more yet to be discovered.

Octopuses, squids, and cuttlefish are cephalopods.

CUTTLEFISH have three hearts, eight arms, and blue-green blood. They can change their shape to look like underwater plants or rocks. They can change their color, too. And they can spew out ink that forms the same shape as their bodies. This really confuses their predators.

Octopuses have organs in their skin that tell them when the water gets lighter or darker. Then their skin changes color to blend in.

● Squids have three hearts. ● Squids have eight arms and two tentacles. Like octopuses, they grow another arm if they lose one. ● Female giant squids are larger than males. ● Squid is a big part of a sperm whale's diet. Sperm whales might eat up to 800 of them a day.

Blue whales are the biggest animals that have ever lived on the planet.

They can weigh over 160 tons and be 100 feet long.

Their tongues weigh about 15,000 pounds! That makes their tongues about twice as heavy as a hippopotamus and the same weight as an elephant or a small car!

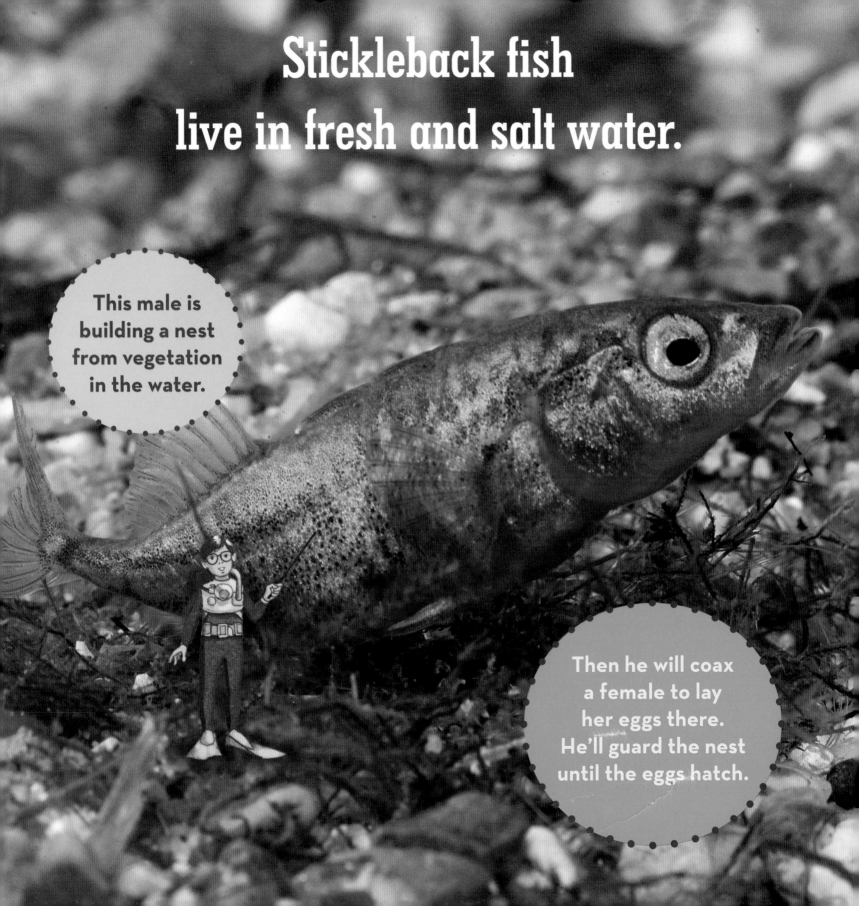

The smallest **SEA HORSE** is only half an inch long.

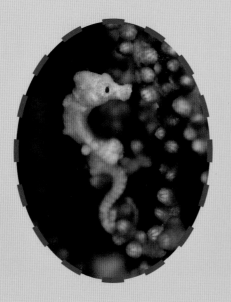

• A sea snake can hold its breath for up to three hours. • In the eastern Himalayas, scientists have recently discovered a fish that can breathe air and stay alive out of water for four days.

The ancient Greeks thought dolphins were messengers from Poseidon, the god of the sea. It was against the law for anyone to hurt a **DOLPHIN**.

Eels are fish that look like long snakes. They wrap themselves around their prey and **SQUEEZE** it until it is flat enough to eat.

There are over 400 different species of sharks.

Sharks can hear movement in the water from 700 feet away.

When sharks are attacking their prey, their teeth move forward so they can get a firm grasp on it.

The most dangerous sharks are the:

MAKO

BULL

TIGER

HAMMERHEAD

GREAT WHITE

People have found all kinds of things in tiger sharks' stomachs: tin cans, old tires, horses, seabirds, and plastic containers!

● **Cookie-cutter sharks take round bites out of other sea creatures. They even bite great whites.** ● **The Tequesta tribe, which lived in Florida, sometimes used shark teeth for spear points and tools.** ● Sharks always keep moving to force oxygen over their gills into their bloodstream. If they don't move, they will suffocate. ● **Sharks have such a great sense of smell that they're able to track prey that is a mile away.** ● Most shark attacks happen less than a hundred feet from the shore, between two o'clock and three o'clock in the afternoon. ● **The first sharks appeared over sixty-four million years ago.** ● A photographer took a picture of a great white shark that was about twenty feet long. That's the largest ever seen.

THE HUMAN BODY

The human brain controls everything that goes on in the body. It works faster than any computer.

• **Billions of neurons in the brain receive messages from all over the body.** • Messages from muscles go about 200 miles per hour. • **Our brains are more active at night than during the day.** • An adult brain weighs about three pounds. • **It's possible for a person's brain to store over one million billion pieces of information in a lifetime.**

If all the blood vessels in our brains were stretched out, they would be 100,000 miles long.

That's about four times around Earth!

Our left lung is **SMALLER** than our right to leave room for the heart.

We breathe in oxygen and breathe out carbon dioxide. We can take in 2,400 gallons of oxygen a day. Each lung contains thirty million air sacs. The total surface area of the air sacs inside the lungs would cover a tennis court.

More than **SIX MILLION** children in the United States have asthma. In an asthma attack, the airways to the lungs get narrower, making it harder to breathe.

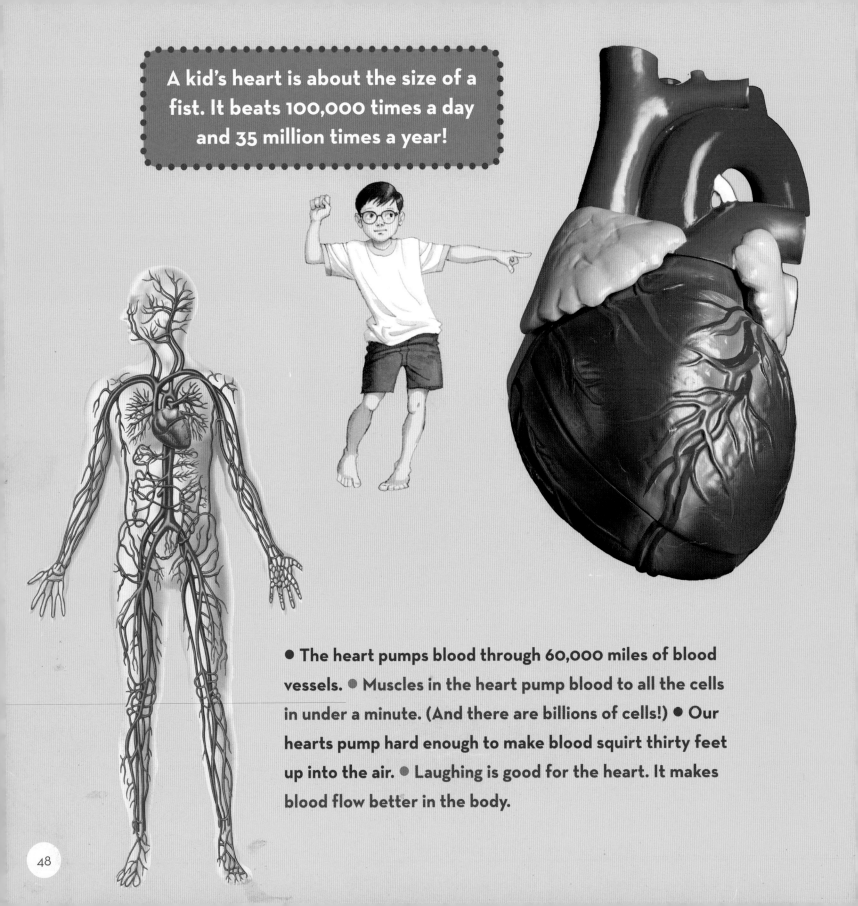

A kid's heart is about the size of a fist. It beats 100,000 times a day and 35 million times a year!

• The heart pumps blood through 60,000 miles of blood vessels. • Muscles in the heart pump blood to all the cells in under a minute. (And there are billions of cells!) • Our hearts pump hard enough to make blood squirt thirty feet up into the air. • Laughing is good for the heart. It makes blood flow better in the body.

BLOOD brings food and oxygen to cells. It also removes waste from them.

Human blood is red because of a protein in it called hemoglobin.

IRON in hemoglobin helps make red blood cells. The body has enough iron in it to make a nail three inches long.

You get a **BRUISE** when you hit something hard enough to break blood vessels under your skin.

Adult bodies usually have over a gallon of blood in them.

Adults have 260 bones.

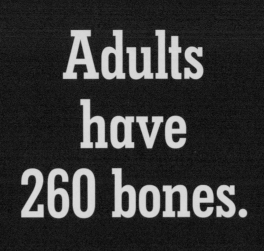

The spine is made up of thirty-three bones.

The femur, or thighbone, is the largest bone in the human body.

● Babies have 320 bones, sixty more than adults. Their bones fuse together as they grow. ● Bones are made mostly of a mineral called calcium. ● Bones are about 31 percent water. ● Over half the bones humans have are in their hands and feet. ● The stapes bone in the ear is the smallest bone in the body. It is only about the length of a grain of rice, but we couldn't hear without it.

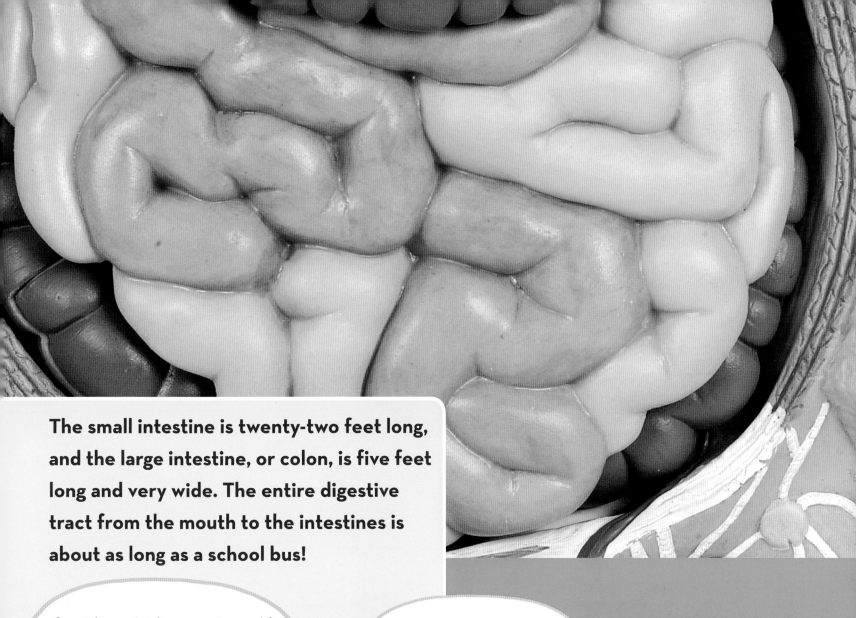

The small intestine is twenty-two feet long, and the large intestine, or colon, is five feet long and very wide. The entire digestive tract from the mouth to the intestines is about as long as a school bus!

But I'm only four and a half feet tall! How could my digestive tract be so long?

Your intestines are coiled up inside you.

It takes about three days for someone to digest a big Thanksgiving dinner.

51

The eye has about 2 million working parts.

Eye muscles are the most **ACTIVE** muscles in the body. The human eye can see 10 million colors.

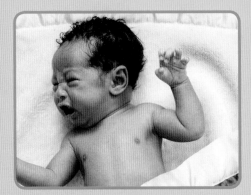

Although newborn babies cry, they don't cry **TEARS** until they're several weeks old.

Blinking cleans and moisturizes the eyes and keeps them from drying out. People blink about twenty times a minute and 10,000 times a day.

The ancient Mayan people of Mexico thought that **CROSSED EYES** looked nice. They attached a ball to a baby's hair so that the child's eyes turned in to see it. The result: long ago, many Mayans were cross-eyed.

Humans can smell over 10,000 different scents.

- People have 10 million scent receptors in their noses.
- A sneeze travels about 100 miles per hour.
- People can't sneeze with their eyes open.
- Everyone has his or her own special smell, except identical twins, who smell alike.
- Hairs inside our noses filter out germs and dust.
- If you get a nosebleed, lean forward a little and pinch the soft part of your nose together with your fingers. Hold it for ten minutes, and the bleeding should stop.

- Touch is the first sense that babies develop in the womb. • Our skin has about five million touch receptors. Each fingerprint has 3,000! • There are two main types of touch receptors. Some feel hot or cold; others can pick up on pressure and texture.

- Humans have between 5,000 and 10,000 taste buds. Most are on our tongues, but there are also taste buds all over the mouth and throat. • There are five main tastes humans can pick up on: sweet, salty, sour, bitter, and umami—a Japanese word for a savory, meaty flavor. • The sense of taste evolved to help animals, including humans, avoid poisons. Most poisons have a bitter or sour taste.

- The inner ear is about the same size around as a pencil eraser. The inner ear is filled with tiny hairs. If we didn't have those hairs, we wouldn't be able to hear. • As people get older, it gets harder for them to hear high-pitched sounds. There is a high-pitched tone that is very annoying to young people that most adults over the age of thirty can't hear. • Our ears don't stop hearing even when we're asleep. Our brain just ignores the information when we're sleeping.

On average, people spend about twenty-five years of their lives sleeping. Kids need about **TEN HOURS** of sleep each night to be at their best the next day. Newborn babies sleep between fourteen and seventeen hours per day.

● Do you dream in black-and-white or color? Most people dream in color, but 12 percent of humans tend to dream in black-and-white. Before color television, only 15 percent of people dreamed in color. ● Wounds heal faster when people get enough sleep. ● People tend to be hungrier when they don't get enough sleep.

People who get enough sleep do much **BETTER** on tests than those who get too little.

There are about 650 muscles in a human's body.

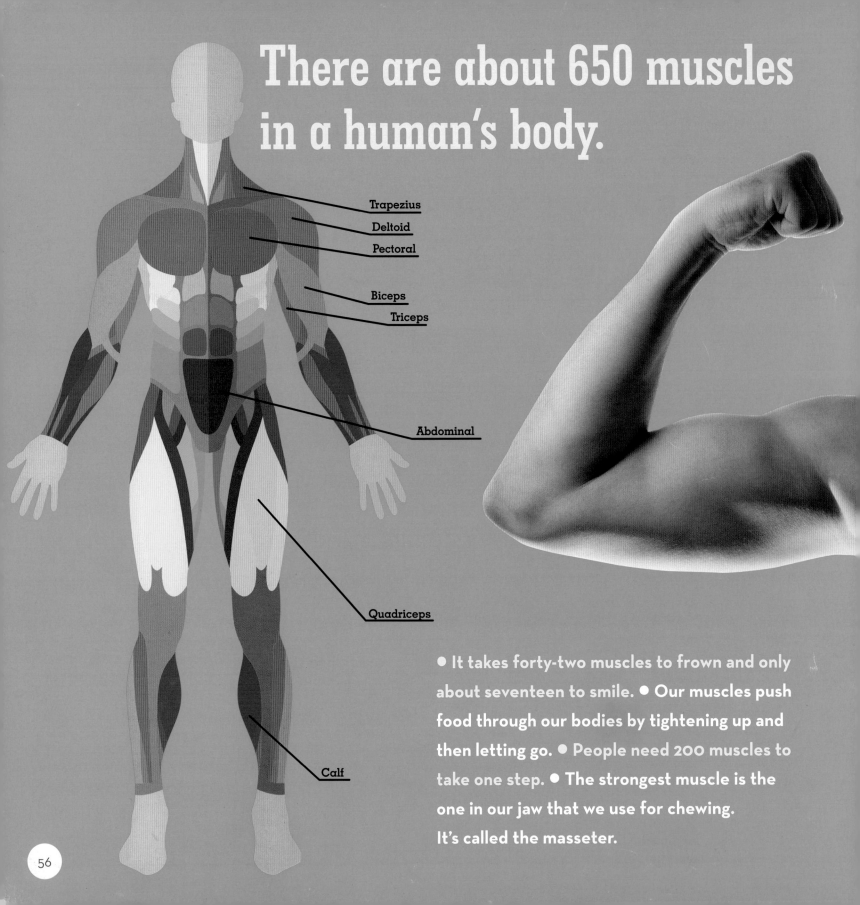

Trapezius

Deltoid

Pectoral

Biceps

Triceps

Abdominal

Quadriceps

Calf

● It takes forty-two muscles to frown and only about seventeen to smile. ● Our muscles push food through our bodies by tightening up and then letting go. ● People need 200 muscles to take one step. ● The strongest muscle is the one in our jaw that we use for chewing. It's called the masseter.

No two people, not even identical twins, have exactly the same **FINGERPRINTS.** It's not just our fingerprints that are one-of-a-kind, though. Every person's tongue has its own special pattern, too.

When we eat, saliva in our mouths makes food wet enough to swallow. Throughout their lifetimes, humans create enough saliva to fill two swimming pools.

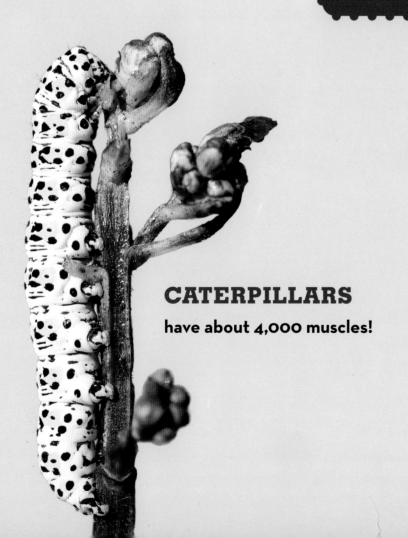

CATERPILLARS

have about 4,000 muscles!

When we shiver from the cold, our muscles contract and relax. These actions give off heat to help keep us warm.

Although humans have billions of cells in their bodies, they have ten times as many bacteria.

People have the same number of hairs on their bodies as chimpanzees. Most human hairs are so small and fine that they're difficult to see.

An adult's skin weighs an average of eight pounds.

People have about 10 trillion skin cells. (That's 10,000,000,000,000!)

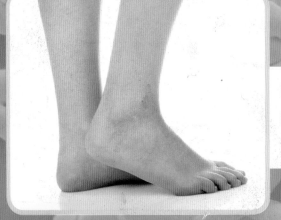

People sweat to cool their bodies down. When it's really hot, adults sweat one to two quarts of water in an hour. The human foot alone has 250,000 sweat glands.

SPECTACULAR SPACE

The universe is all of space, including the sun, stars, moons, and planets. It's full of dust, rocks, ice, gases, and trillions of miles of empty space.

Every hour, the universe expands billions of miles.

Gravity is the force that pulls things toward each other. If there were no gravity, we would all float up into the sky. No one completely understands what causes gravity. We do know that the more mass an object has, the more gravity it produces.

The sun is a star.

The sun's mass makes up 99.86 percent of the total mass of our solar system.

More than a million Earths could fit inside the sun.

The sun weighs 330,000 times more than Earth.

It is the center of our solar system.

Light travels 186,287 miles per second. It takes a little over eight minutes for light to travel the 93 million miles from the sun to Earth.

We measure space by the distance light travels in one year. This is called a light-year.

One light-year equals 5.88 trillion miles.

Some ancient cultures, including the Egyptians, Aztecs, Norse, Greeks, and Romans, worshipped sun gods.

The planets that orbit the sun are Mercury, Venus, Earth, Mars, Jupiter, Saturn, Uranus, and Neptune.

Earth is the third planet from the sun. It is the **ONLY** planet known to have both oxygen and water. It is just the right distance from the sun to have liquid water. This is one of the most important factors in making life on Earth possible.

Because the gravity is different on different planets, people would not weigh the same as they do on Earth. A 60-pound kid would weigh 22.6 pounds on Mercury and Mars, 54.4 on Venus, 141.8 on Jupiter, 63.8 on Saturn, 53.3 on Uranus, and 67.5 on Neptune.

Jupiter, Saturn, Uranus, and Neptune are mostly made up of gases. There is no solid ground on Jupiter at all, just gas.

Earth's solar system began over 4.6 million years ago. • It is made up of the sun and eight planets plus their moons. • Planets orbit around the sun. • Planets travel around the sun at different speeds. • One trip around the sun is a planet's year. • Planets also rotate, or spin, as they move around the sun. • One rotation is the planet's day. • Earth goes around the sun at about 67,000 miles per hour. We don't feel it because the speed stays constant.

Saturn, Jupiter, Uranus, and Neptune have rings around them.

The three largest rings of Saturn are mostly made up of ice particles.

Some particles in Saturn's rings are as small as grains of sand. Others are several yards long.

VENUS is the hottest planet, even though Mercury is closer to the sun. This is because it has a thick atmosphere with lots of carbon dioxide in it to hold in the heat. The average temperature on Venus is 864 degrees Fahrenheit.

MERCURY is 801 degrees Fahrenheit during the day and 279 degrees below zero at night. One day on Mercury is equal to 59 days on Earth.

NEPTUNE has fourteen moons. Triton, its largest, orbits backward around the planet. Jet-stream winds on Neptune blow about 1,500 miles per hour. That's five times faster than the strongest wind ever recorded on Earth.

Mercury, Venus, Earth, and Mars are made of rocks and metals.

It's raining **DIAMONDS** on Jupiter and Saturn.

Carbon gas surrounds the planets. Lightning changes some of the gas into diamond **RAINFALLS.**

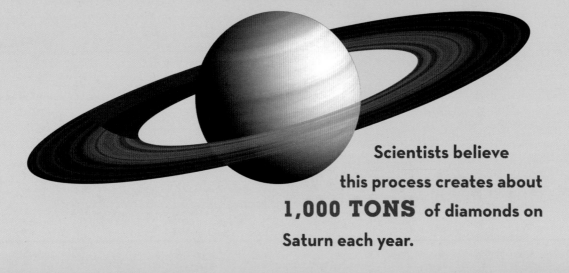

Scientists believe this process creates about **1,000 TONS** of diamonds on Saturn each year.

The **GREAT RED SPOT** on Jupiter is actually a storm that was first discovered 300 years ago. It has continued ever since. But scientists say that the spot is now more orange than red, and they think the storm is dying down.

Jupiter has **MORE MOONS** than any other planet. Sixty-seven have been discovered, and there may be more.

Because Mars has a red glow, it's called the Red Planet.

Its color comes from rust on the planet's rocks.

Mars has the highest mountain of any planet. It's called Olympus Mons and is **THREE TIMES AS TALL** as Mount Everest.

There is a **VALLEY** on Mars that is five to six miles deep and 2,500 miles long.

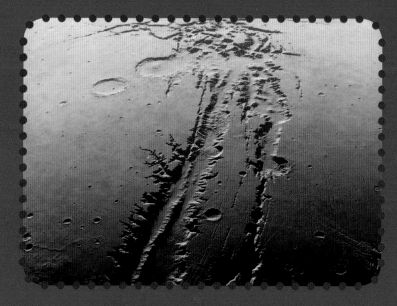

Billions of years ago, Mars may have had rivers and oceans. In a recent discovery, scientists learned that **WATER** lies trapped under the ice caps at its north and south poles.

Dust storms on Mars cover the entire planet and can last for many months.

A dwarf planet is smaller than a regular planet.

It does not have enough gravity to keep smaller objects out of its orbit. The five known dwarf planets in our solar system are:

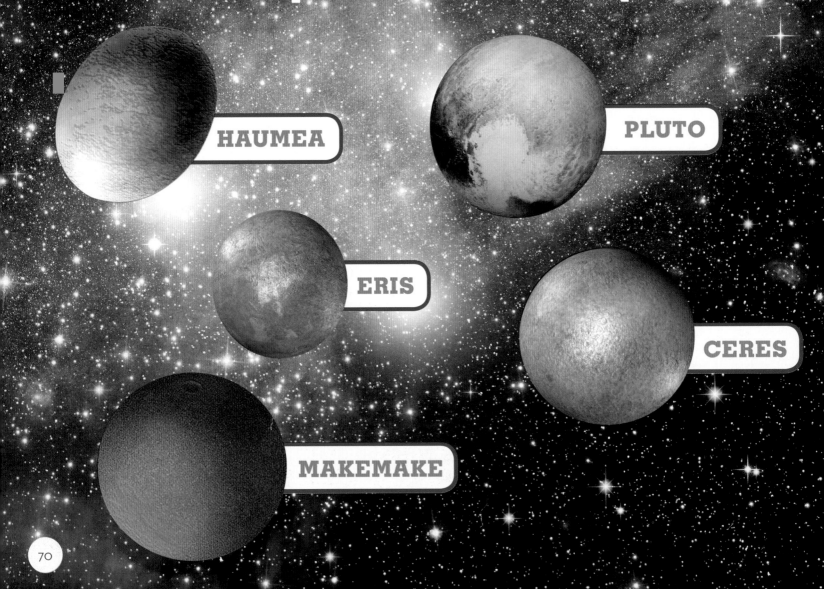

HAUMEA

PLUTO

ERIS

CERES

MAKEMAKE

Pluto used to be called a planet.

In 2006, astronomers decided it was more similar to other dwarf planets, so now they consider it a dwarf planet, too.

When Pluto was discovered in 1930, Venetia Burney, an eleven-year-old English girl, named it. This icy, dark planet was so far away from the sun that it reminded her of Pluto, **GREEK GOD** of the underworld.

Comets are balls of ice, dust, and rock.

● When the sun begins to melt them, dust and gases can form a tail that we sometimes see when a comet streaks across the sky. ● The word *comet* comes from the Greek word *kometes*, which means "head with long hair." ● The longest comet tail ever recorded was observed in 1843. It was almost 500 million miles long—the distance from Earth to Jupiter.

Meteors are rocks and other objects in outer space. They often hit Earth, although most of them are very small. When they hit, they are called meteorites. Meteors that fly into Earth's atmosphere and fly out again are known as **EARTH-GRAZING FIREBALLS.**

In 1948, a huge fireball crashed in a Nebraska field. It was a big meteorite, weighing over 2,000 pounds, that buried itself ten feet down in the dirt.

One of the **BIGGEST** meteorite craters on Earth is in Arizona. It is almost a mile across.

No one knows how many stars
are in the **UNIVERSE.**

Space is nearly
silent to the
human ear.

A **GALAXY** is made up of
millions of stars that are all held
together by gravity. There are about
100 billion galaxies.

The galaxy that our sun occupies is called the Milky Way.

The sun travels around the entire galaxy once every 200 million years. If you traveled away from Earth at 100 miles per hour, it would take 221 million years to get to the center of the Milky Way.

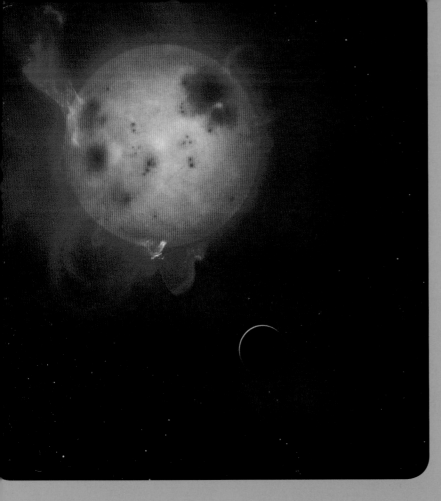

The most common kind of star is a **RED DWARF**. Red dwarfs are small and cool compared to other stars. They aren't bright enough to be seen from Earth without a telescope. Stars get their energy from burning hydrogen. Red dwarfs burn through their hydrogen slowly, so they can last trillions of years.

A star like the sun lasts around 10 billion years. After it burns through all the hydrogen at its core, it expands to become a red giant. As it fades away, it becomes a **WHITE DWARF.** Dying stars are very dense. One teaspoon of material from a white dwarf star could weigh up to 100 tons.

A **BLACK HOLE** comes from a large star that has burned out and collapsed in on itself. Everything in a black hole is so tightly packed together that it has superpowerful gravity. Anything that comes near it gets pulled toward its center. Nothing can escape from a black hole, not even light.

Although black holes are different sizes, some are many times **BIGGER** than the sun.

Gravity on the moon is much less than it is on Earth.

Because of this, you can't really walk on it like you would on Earth.

It's easier to hop than to walk!

The pull of the moon's gravity causes high and low tides in the ocean. The most extreme tides are in the **BAY OF FUNDY** in Canada. There can be as much as a fifty-three-foot difference between high and low tides.

The moon weighs 81 billion tons. There is no water, air, or wind on the gray rocky surface of the moon.

A **SOLAR ECLIPSE** takes place when the moon is between Earth and the sun.

Astronauts left their **FOOTPRINTS** behind when they walked on the moon. Since there is no wind there, the footprints will last for millions of years.

SUPER SCIENCE AND NATURE

• Clouds are made of water and air. • Wind is moving air. • When warm air rises and colder air moves in to take its place, wind is created. • Wind doesn't make any noise unless it hits an object.

The wind can be a very **POWERFUL** source of energy. Windmills use the power of the wind to make machines work. The earliest known windmill was invented in ancient Greece. By the Middle Ages in Europe, windmills for grinding grain were common.

Wind power is a clean source of energy. Today, huge wind turbines generate energy. Large groups of **WIND TURBINES** are called wind farms. The world's biggest wind farm is in China.

Tornadoes have winds of up to 300 miles per hour.

STORM CLOUDS are made up of wind, water droplets, and ice crystals that move up and down with great force. The movement within a storm cloud creates the huge electrical sparks that cause lightning. Lightning strikes the earth about 100 times every second.

● There are 45,000 thunderstorms all over the world every day. ● Florida has an average of 1.45 million lightning strikes a year—more than any other place in the United States. ● Tampa, Florida, is especially known for its lightning strikes. The name *Tampa* came from an ancient American Indian tribe called the Calusa. In their language, Tampa meant "sticks of fire." ● A bolt of lightning can be more than five times hotter than the surface of the sun.

HURRICANES start over the ocean with groups of thunderstorms near the equator. Hurricanes are the most dangerous storms, with winds that can reach 150 miles per hour. They can last for several days and cover thousands of miles. In 1970, a hurricane in Pakistan killed more than 500,000 people.

Most waves are caused by wind. But not tsunamis.

Tsunamis are a series of waves that travel across the ocean faster than a jet plane and hit the shore with deadly force.

Tsunamis often begin with earthquakes, landslides, or volcanic eruptions beneath the sea.

In 2004, a tsunami began when a volcano erupted in the Indian Ocean. More than 300,000 people died.

Earth is about 4.54 billion years old.

Earth's inner core is a mixture of iron and nickel, with a temperature of **5,000 DEGREES.** (That's only 778 degrees cooler than the sun!)

Seventy percent of the planet is covered in water.

The oceans contain millions of tons of **GOLD.**

There are deep
SALTWATER LAKES
on the ocean floor. Some
are 300 feet deep, with
many different kinds of sea
creatures living in them.

• The two biggest oceans are the Atlantic
and the Pacific. • The Atlantic Ocean covers
about 21 percent of Earth. It is saltier than
the Pacific Ocean. • The Pacific is the largest
ocean, covering 30 percent of the world's
surface. • The word *pacific* means "peaceful."

There are **25,000
ISLANDS** in the
Pacific Ocean.

The largest mountain range on the planet is actually underwater. It's a chain of volcanoes in the Pacific Ocean called the Ring of Fire, and it extends 40,389 miles.

Japan has 200 volcanoes, more than any other country.

Sixty of them are active. The Japanese experience about 1,500 earthquakes a year. Most don't cause a lot of damage.

There are rain forests all over the world.

More than half of all the different kinds of plants on Earth grow in rain forests.

Almost all rain forests get at least six feet of rain every year. Some get as much as thirty feet!

The Amazon rain forest covers 1.4 billion acres in nine different countries in South America: Brazil, Peru, Colombia, Venezuela, Ecuador, Bolivia, Suriname, Guyana, and French Guiana. ● It is the largest tropical rain forest in the world. It gives off 20 percent of the world's oxygen. ● Researchers say that there are millions of species in the Amazon rain forest still to be discovered.

The Amazon rain forest contains:

430 ANIMAL SPECIES

40,000 PLANT SPECIES

2.5 MILLION INSECT SPECIES

1,300 BIRD SPECIES

3,000 FISH SPECIES

The Arctic is the northernmost part of the Earth. Although it is very cold there, many animals make it their home.

POLAR BEARS

WHALES

SEALS

WALRUSES

FOXES

The Arctic includes parts of different countries, including the United States (Alaska), Canada, Russia, Finland, Denmark, Iceland, and Sweden.

About **10 PERCENT** of the world's freshwater is frozen in the Arctic.

The **TUNDRA** in the Arctic is land that is flat and frozen with no trees.

In spite of its poor soil and lack of rain, over **1,700 PLANT SPECIES** grow in the Arctic tundra.

People can't live without plants.

• Plants get energy from the sun and turn it into food. • All animals need oxygen. Plants take in carbon dioxide and give off oxygen. • There are more than 80,000 edible plants. Most of our food comes from just thirty of them. • We use over 70,000 plants for medicine.

Because they contain seeds, avocados, eggplant, cucumbers, tomatoes, squash, peppers, olives, and pumpkins are **FRUITS**, not vegetables.

STRAWBERRIES
are the only fruits that have
seeds on the outside.

Apple seeds contain
a poison called
CYANIDE.

Munching on just one
BUTTERCUP
will make a cow sick.

But don't worry! You would
have to eat about 145 seeds
before getting sick. And you
would have to chew them
a lot. Your body can't break
down the hard coating on
apple seeds.

95

Wind, water, fire, and animals help spread seeds to different places.

Winds can carry dandelion seeds for 500 miles.

Australia has a lot of **WILDFIRES.** Some plants there release their seeds only when fire heats the air around them.

The tallest tree in the world is the coast redwood of California. It can grow up to 360 feet tall.

Bamboo is a **GRASS** and not a tree. It can grow thirty-five inches in one day.

● Most oak trees don't produce acorns until they're about fifty years old. ● The trees can live for 200 years. ● About a hundred different animals, including deer, bears, squirrels, ducks, chipmunks, and blue jays, depend on acorns for food, especially as the weather starts to get cold. ● Seventy percent of the white-tailed deer's diet is made up of acorns.

Sundew plants prey on insects.

Their leaves have tentacles with sticky hairs that shine like dewdrops.

When an insect lands on the plant to sip nectar, it gets stuck. The tentacles curl over and smother it. Then the sundew will take several weeks to digest its meal.

Flowers on the **SPIDERWORT PLANT** change colors depending on the levels of pollution in the air.

SUNFLOWERS grow eight to twelve feet tall in six months. After nuclear disasters occurred in Russia and Japan, people planted millions of sunflowers to help take up toxins from the soil.

The **CORPSE FLOWER** of Sumatra grows ten feet tall and has a stem that can weigh 100 pounds. The heaviest stem ever recorded was 258 pounds. Corpse flowers grow for seven to ten years before they bloom. The stench of the plant's red flowers has been compared to rotting meat, dirty diapers, and dead animals. The corpse flower's blossom lasts only about forty-eight hours. (Thank goodness!)

Fossil fuels come from fossils of animals and plants that lived and died over 500 million years ago, before dinosaurs roamed Earth.

Oil and natural gas come from the fossils of **DEAD ANIMALS.**

Coal comes from the fossils of **PLANTS.**

MERCURY is the only metal that is liquid at room temperature.

Hot water freezes faster than cold water.

If you mix the right amount of **CORNSTARCH AND WATER** together, strange things happen. When you squeeze it, it feels solid because the cornstarch molecules squeeze tightly together. If you push your finger into it slowly, the mix is soft and seems to be a liquid. That's because the cornstarch molecules have had time to move away from one another.

The chemical symbol for water is H_2O. That is because water molecules are made of two atoms of hydrogen and one atom of oxygen.

- An element is something made from just one kind of atom and can't be broken down into anything smaller.
- Scientists have discovered about 120 elements. Among them are iron, copper, oxygen, hydrogen, gold, sulfur, and silver.

If you put salt into water, the water level goes down instead of up.

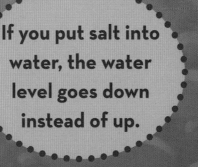

When baking soda and vinegar are mixed together, a **CHEMICAL REACTION** makes the mixture bubble and fizz.

Hydrogen is the most common element.

Distilled
VINEGAR

Pure
aking Soda

Calcium burns with an orange flame, boron produces a green flame, strontium burns red, copper burns blue, and sodium is yellow.

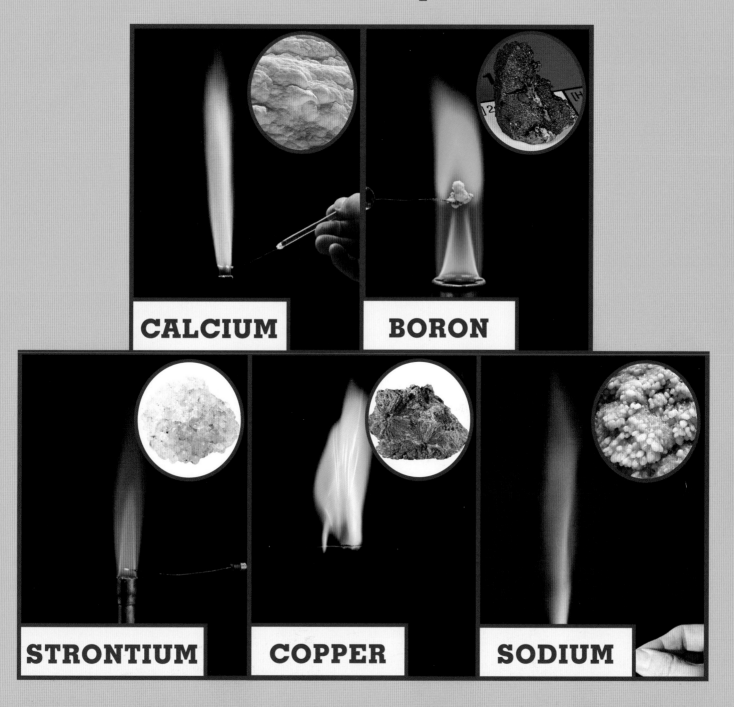

CALCIUM

BORON

STRONTIUM

COPPER

SODIUM

AROUND THE WORLD

There are fifty-four countries in Africa, more than any other continent. Between 800 and 2,000 languages are spoken in Africa.

Victoria Falls, on the border of Zambia and Zimbabwe, is the largest waterfall on Earth.

The **SAHARA DESERT** covers most of the northern part of Africa. It's the largest desert in the world—bigger than the continental United States!

● Chimpanzees, giraffes, gorillas, hippopotamuses, wildebeests, and zebras are found in the wild only in Africa. ● The African elephant is the largest land animal. ● The world's longest river is the Nile. Eleven African countries depend on water from the Nile. ● Many of the best runners are Kenyan. Men and women from Kenya won the New York City, London, Chicago, and Berlin marathons in 2015.

Some of the oldest Christian churches are in **ETHIOPIA.** Many of them are carved out of rock, some high up on cliffs. People have to climb to reach them.

Asia is the largest continent, both in area and in number of people who live there.

People come from all over the world to visit the Great Wall of China. It covers more than 13,000 miles. The oldest part dates from around 700 BCE.

● China has more people than any other country—over 1.3 billion. ● In China, there is a special soup made out of edible birds' nests. ● **Hong Kong is the skyscraper capital of the world. It has over 8,000 buildings that are more than fourteen stories high, double the number in New York City.** ● The biggest traffic jam ever was in China. It was sixty miles long and lasted ten days! ● **China owns all the giant pandas on the planet. Pandas in zoos around the world are rented from China.**

- On average, Japanese people live longer than any other people. - Japanese farmers grow square watermelons so they can stack them neatly in stores. - Elderly people are honored all year long in Japan, but they also have their own national holiday, Respect for the Aged Day.

- In Tibet, people sometimes greet each other by sticking out their tongues. - In Pohang, Korea, some prisons use robots as guards. - The earliest known civilization was in ancient Mesopotamia, which is now Iraq. - One of the world's most famous archaeological sites is the rock-hewn desert city of Petra in Jordan. Only about 15 percent of it has been uncovered so far. - The highest mountains in the world—the Himalayas—are in Asia.

- There are over 780 different languages spoken in India. - Four of the world's major religions began in India: Hinduism, Jainism, Buddhism, and Sikhism. - There are more vegetarians in India than in any other country. - India is known for its many festivals. Some popular ones are snake, camel, and kite festivals. - Chess was invented in India. - Yoga has been practiced in India for 5,000 years. - Martial arts began in India.

Russia is in both Europe and Asia. In area, it is the largest country in the world.

Many old Russian buildings have domes that look like brightly painted onions. One of the best known is St. Basil's Cathedral in Moscow.

● In the city of Moscow, stray dogs have learned how to get around on the subways. ● Many European countries share the same money, the euro. ● The Vatican, which is home to the pope, lies within the city of Rome, Italy. It is the smallest country in the world—about one-eighth the size of Central Park in New York City. ● Italy has more UNESCO World Heritage sites than any other country. UNESCO is a United Nations group that recognizes historically or culturally important places.

WINDSOR CASTLE

in England is the biggest royal home in the world. The British royal family has lived there since 1080.

● Most families in Finland relax in their own saunas at home. ● Schoolkids in Finland do better on tests than any schoolkids anywhere. And their teachers give them little if any homework. ● More tourists visit France than any other country in the world. Many of them go to the Louvre in Paris, the world's most visited art museum. Leonardo da Vinci's famous painting *Mona Lisa* is on display there.

Iceland has many hot springs and **GEYSERS.** In fact, the word *geyser* comes from the earliest known geyser, Iceland's Geysir.

Australia, New Zealand, Fiji, Micronesia, Papua New Guinea, Samoa, and several smaller island nations make up a region called Oceania.

● Vegetation covers 91 percent of Australia.
● Eighty percent of the plants and animals in Australia can't be found anywhere else. ● Kangaroos, emus, koalas, wombats, dingoes, platypuses, and Tasmanian devils are all unique to Australia. ● There are more kangaroos in Australia than people. ● Australia's Great Barrier Reef is the largest coral reef in the world.

The **BOOMERANG** comes from Australia. Native Australian people used it for hunting.

The clearest freshwater on Earth is in the **BLUE LAKE** in New Zealand.

The **KIWI,** a bird that cannot fly, lives only in New Zealand. It has become a symbol of the country, and people from New Zealand are sometimes called Kiwis.

● Between 1888 and 1912, a dolphin named Pelorus Jack guided ships through the dangerous waters of Cook Strait in New Zealand. ● A hill in Hawke Bay, New Zealand, has the longest place name anywhere. It's called:

Taumatawhakatangihangakoauauotamateaturipu-kakapikimaungahoronukupokaiwhenuakitanatahu.

Wow! That's eighty-five letters!

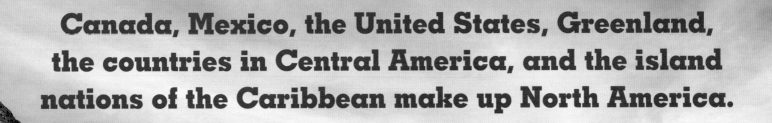

Canada, Mexico, the United States, Greenland, the countries in Central America, and the island nations of the Caribbean make up North America.

The hottest recorded temperature was in Death Valley, California, in 1913. It reached 134 degrees Fahrenheit on July 10 that year.

• People first came to North America during the Ice Age. • North America has every climate type, from desert to tundra to tropical rain forests.

• Yellowstone National Park, mostly in the states of Montana and Wyoming, was the world's first national park. It was created in 1872, before Montana and Wyoming were even states. Yellowstone has more than 300 geysers and 290 waterfalls.

There are more lakes in **CANADA** than in all other countries combined.

● **Canada has the longest coastline in the world.** ● Canada has won more gold medals at a single Winter Olympics than any other country. In Vancouver in 2010, Canadians won fourteen gold medals. ● **November 1 is a special holiday in Mexico called the Day of the Dead. Families go to cemeteries and have picnics on their relatives' graves.** ● Chocolate and popcorn are both from Mexico.

The **LARGEST PYRAMID** in the world is in Mexico, not in Egypt. It is known as the Great Pyramid of Cholula, and the oldest part dates from around 200 BCE. It was a temple to the Aztec god Quetzalcoatl.

The Andes Mountains in South America are the longest mountain range in the world. They are also the second tallest.

Llamas, alpacas, and chinchillas live in the Andes.

The Inca ruins of **MACHU PICCHU** in Peru are amazing! A whole complex of stone buildings seems to cling to the remote mountainside. The wheel had not been invented in Inca society. Yet Inca builders managed to haul huge granite blocks up the mountain without the wheel. They used terraces to make the buildings safe in case of landslides.

● The highest waterfall in the world is Angel Falls in Venezuela. ● The Galápagos Islands are part of Ecuador. They are home to the Galápagos tortoise, the largest tortoise and longest-living vertebrate on Earth. ● Some Galápagos tortoises have lived to be more than 150 years old. ● In 1835, Charles Darwin visited the Galápagos Islands. He discovered that different islands in the chain had unique species of birds and tortoises. This was a major step toward his theory of evolution.

EASTER ISLAND is a Polynesian island that is part of Chile. It is famous for the hundreds of giant stone heads dating from between 1250 and 1500 that jut up from its hills. But they are more than just heads! The statues have been buried up to their shoulders, but they do have bodies. No one is sure why the statues were created.

SPORTS

Venus Williams, one of the world's greatest tennis players, began playing when she was only four.

The **LONGEST** tennis match ever was in 2010 at the Wimbledon tennis tournament in England. John Isner and Nicolas Mahut played for three days, with a total playing time of eleven hours. Isner won.

Over the years it's been the custom for tennis players to wear white clothes to hide their sweat stains. Professional players must wear white to compete in Wimbledon.

When **WOMEN** first played tennis in 1860, they wore long-sleeved dresses that went down to their ankles.

In 1989, a **LIGHTNING** strike killed an entire eleven-person soccer team in the Democratic Republic of the Congo. Although some members of the other team were injured, none of them died.

Greenland can't compete in FIFA soccer because there isn't enough grass in the country for soccer fields.

There is a beautiful arch in Paris called the **ARC DE TRIOMPHE.** A flame constantly burns there to honor French soldiers who have died in battle. One of the few times the flame has ever gone out was when a Mexican soccer fan peed on it after the 1998 World Cup hosted by France.

In 1914, German and English armies fighting each other in World War I called a **CHRISTMAS TRUCE.** The soldiers gave each other presents and took time off for a soccer match.

In the United States, people watch football more than any other sport.

● In the 1972 football season, the Miami Dolphins never lost a game. This is an NFL record. ● The Pittsburgh Steelers have won six Super Bowls, the most ever. The Dallas Cowboys and the San Francisco 49ers have each won five. ● NFL stadiums are always built facing north and south so the sun won't get in the players' eyes.

The average height of NFL
QUARTERBACKS
is between six feet one inch
and six feet two inches.

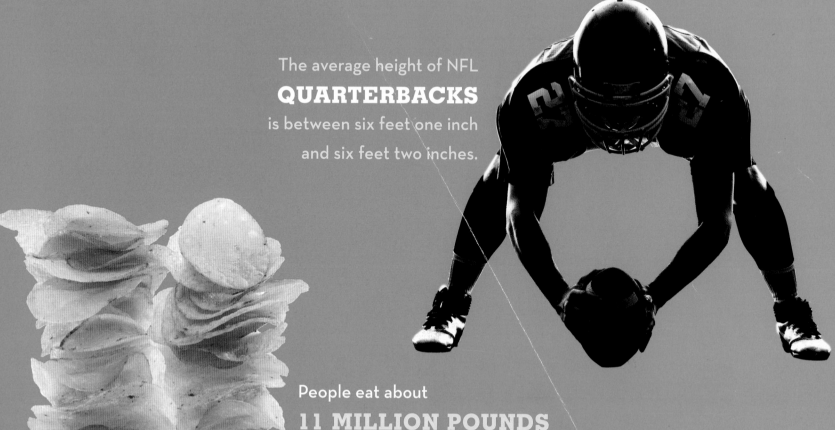

People eat about
11 MILLION POUNDS
of chips on Super Bowl Sunday.

Olympic gold medals are mostly silver covered in a thin layer of gold.

ABEBE BIKILA from Ethiopia was a marathon winner in the 1960 Rome Olympics. He ran the entire race barefoot.

The average downhill skier goes between ten and twenty miles per hour. Olympic skiers like **LINDSEY VONN** go as fast as ninety-five miles per hour.

Dimitrios Loundras, a Greek gymnast, was the youngest person ever in the Olympics. He won a bronze medal at the 1896 Games when he was only ten! The youngest gold medalist was **MARJORIE GESTRING,** a diver from the United States. She won in 1936 when she was thirteen.

The tallest basketball players to ever play in the NBA both measure seven feet seven inches tall. They are:

MANUTE BOL

GHEORGHE MURESAN

● During his baseball career, Barry Bonds hit 762 home runs. That's more than anyone else in professional baseball. ● Aroldis Chapman, a major league pitcher, threw a pitch clocked at 106 miles per hour. ● A baseball player can swing a bat up to 80 miles per hour!

In 1971, astronaut Alan Shepard smuggled a golf club and two balls on his spaceship. He was the first person ever to play **GOLF** on the moon.

FAMOUS LANDMARKS

With the help of 400 workers, a sculptor named Gutzon Borglum and his son carved huge heads of George Washington, Thomas Jefferson, Theodore Roosevelt, and Abraham Lincoln on the side of Mount Rushmore. The whole project took about fourteen years. Each of the heads is as tall as six-story building. The mouths are eighteen feet wide, and their noses are twenty feet long.

Because the White House was finished after George Washington's presidency, he never lived there. John Adams, the second president of the United States, was the first president to live in the White House.

The White House has thirty-five bathrooms.

The U.S. Capitol has its own **SUBWAY** system that connects the Capitol to the House and Senate office buildings.

Skyscrapers are built to sway back and forth in strong winds to protect them from damage.

The Empire State Building is struck by lightning about twenty-three times per year.

The Empire State Building was built in 1931, and for forty years, it was the tallest building in the world.

It took 10 million bricks to build it.

Today the tallest building in the world is the Burj Khalifa in Dubai. It is 2,717 feet tall and has 163 floors.

It took over 2.3 million stone blocks, most weighing two tons, to build the **GREAT PYRAMID OF GIZA.**

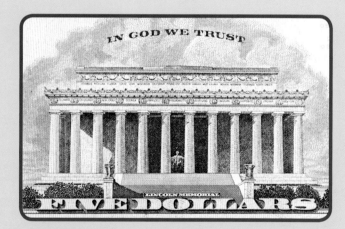

There is a picture of the **LINCOLN MEMORIAL** on the back of the five-dollar bill. If you look carefully, you'll see the names of twenty-six states on the front of the building.

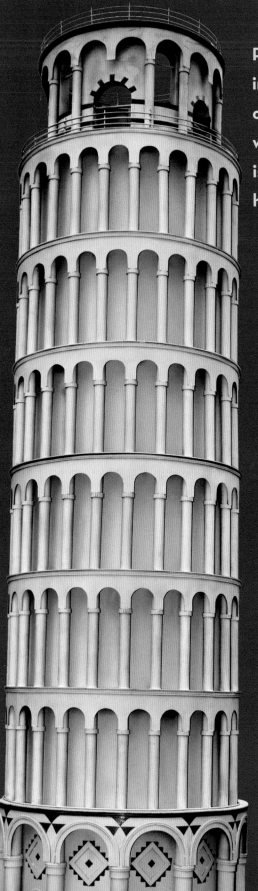

People began building the **LEANING TOWER OF PISA** in Italy in 1173 and continued working on it for 300 years. One side of the tower is built on soil that is too soft to support the building's weight. The side that doesn't lean is 187.27 feet high. The leaning side is 186 feet high. In 2008, engineers concluded that the Leaning Tower has stopped moving. Yay!

Each winter since 1989, there has been an **ICE HOTEL** in Sweden. Everything—the walls, the beds, the furniture—is made entirely of ice. In the spring, the ice melts, so the hotel must be constructed again every year. Now there are also ice hotels in Canada, Finland, Japan, Lapland, Norway, and Romania.

The **EIFFEL TOWER** was built in 1889 for the World's Fair in Paris. It was named for its designer, Gustave Eiffel. At the time it was built, many people in France thought it was ugly and wanted it taken down. Today the Eiffel Tower is a beloved symbol of Paris.

MORE COOL FACTS

Coral reefs are home to more animal species than any place on Earth.

Thousands of years ago, people brushed their **TEETH** with things like ground-up ox hooves, bones, and shells.

In the 1600s, rich people in Europe often wore **SIX-INCH RED HIGH HEELS.** They needed a servant on either side to help them walk!

In 2005, people in New York City noticed an odor in the air that was like **MAPLE SYRUP OR CARAMEL.** For several years afterward, the smell would return now and then. Someone discovered that it came from a factory in New Jersey that used seeds from the fenugreek plant to make flavoring for foods.

- Neanderthals had bigger brains than humans do today. • In the Olympic games of ancient Greece, the athletes didn't wear any clothes. • Virginia has produced more American presidents than any other state. • There are twice as many left-handed men as there are left-handed women. • If you're left-handed, the nails on your left hand grow faster than on your right, and vice versa. • If a man never cut his beard, it could grow thirty feet in his lifetime. • Kids grow faster in the spring. • If you yawn, there's a good chance that someone near you will also yawn. • It takes seven minutes for the average person to fall asleep. • The world record for juggling a soccer ball is held by Dan Magness of England. He juggled it for 26 hours! • The word *nerd* was invented by Dr. Seuss, who first used it in his book *If I Ran the Zoo*. • The shortest complete sentence in the English language is "I am."

Waterfall-climbing **CAVEFISH** live in caves in Thailand. They don't have eyes or any pigment in their skin. When they are in fast-moving streams, they use their large fins to climb rocks.

● Ever heard of the "human fish"? That's what scientists call olms—long, flesh-colored, blind salamanders that live deep underwater in caves in Croatia and Slovenia. Some live for a hundred years, which is way longer than any other amphibian. ● African lungfish dig burrows in pools of water. About every thirty minutes they go to the surface to breathe. Lungfish can survive for years without food. ● Male toads croak. Female toads don't. ● Turtles breathe through their mouths, but some, like eastern painted turtles, breathe through their back ends as well! ● Chameleons don't change color to protect themselves. They do it to warn other chameleons of danger. ● Horseshoe crabs have light receptors in their tails. ● Hippos have red and orange pigments in their sweat.

There are more
FAKE FLAMINGOS
in the world than real ones.

GOATS have rectangular pupils.

• A duck's quack never produces an echo. • A bat can eat about a thousand mosquitoes in an hour. • Because of their neck muscles, pigs can't look up at the sky when they're standing. • Forget a red cape! Bulls are color-blind. • Kangaroos can't hop backward. • Cockroaches can live for several weeks without their heads.

The **BASENJI** is the only dog that never barks. Instead, it howls, yodels, and growls.

Only male **TURKEYS** gobble. Females cackle.

• The average pencil can draw a line that's over thirty miles long. • The Statue of Liberty has a thirty-five-foot waistline and wears size 879 shoes. • Every year, about 600 bolts of lightning hit the Statue of Liberty. • On average, the ocean is 12,100 feet deep—that's deeper than eight Empire State Buildings stacked on top of each other.

INDEX